Sleek

Charles Edwin Bolles, *Elmina*, 1901

Charles Edwin Bolles, *Fanny*, 1892

Charles Edwin Bolles, *Gracie*, 1893

5

Charles Edwin Bolles, *Canada* and *Zelma*, 1896

Arthur F. Aldridge, *Constitution* and *Columbia*, 1901

Contents

Sleek

CLASSIC IMAGES FROM THE

ROSENFELD COLLECTION

TEXT BY JOHN ROUSMANIERE

MYSTIC SEAPORT · THE MUSEUM OF AMERICA AND THE SEA

MYSTIC SEAPORT
75 Greenmanville Ave.
P. O. Box 6000
Mystic, CT 06355-0990

First edition

Created and produced by Constance Sullivan/Hummingbird Books

Manufactured in Italy

ISBN 0-939510-90-1

Mystic Seaport—The Museum of America and the Sea—is the nation's leading maritime museum,
presenting the American experience from a maritime perspective.
Located along the banks of the historic Mystic River in Mystic, Connecticut,
the Museum houses extensive collections representing the material culture of maritime America,
and offers educational programs from preschool to postgraduate.

For more information, call us at 888-SEAPORT, or visit us on the Web at
www.mysticseaport.org

Acknowledgments

I would like to thank Connie Sullivan of Hummingbird Books who created this fascinating book and selected the photographs, and Mary Anne Stets, Curator of Photography at Mystic Seaport, for inviting me to write the text, which was copyedited by Andy German and Joe Hannan. Amy German and Victoria Sharps provided research assistance in the museum archive. Tony Peluso, who has been studying the nineteenth-century photographers far longer than I, offered valuable information about them and their community. Bill Watson, librarian at the New York Yacht Club, was, as always, generous with his knowledge, time, and patience as I rummaged around in scrapbooks and books in that remarkable archive. I also conducted research for this book in Avery and Butler libraries at Columbia University and at the New York Public Library.

Charles Edwin Bolles, *Defender*, 1895

Reaching Right into Your Heart

We didn't just "make a photograph." When we snapped the shutter, we had to feel both
intellectually and in our bodies that what we were doing was right.
What motivated us was always the best thing we could see.

STANLEY ROSENFELD

The quote above is from a conversation I once had with the youngest of the five artists whose work is represented in this book, the man who conveyed the Rosenfeld Collection of photographs to Mystic Seaport. His ideal defines this collection of images from the golden age of both yachting and yacht photography between 1890 and 1955.

What exactly was "the best thing we could see"? "When we looked at a boat," Stanley explained about his and his father's approach, "we tried to understand enough about the boat—how the designer meant it to look, how a type of boat evolved, what the function of the boat was—so that the boat appeared in our minds and in our eyes on the camera the way it was *supposed to look*." It is a matter of fit between boat and environment. The boat sails so rightly and intimately in her setting that the water and wind seem made for her, not she for them. You need not be an America's Cup winner or 'round-the-world sailor to have this insight into a right fit. It comes almost instinctively and is felt, as Stanley suggested, to the core of the viewer's being. When the art historian J. Carter Brown praised Olin Stephens's yacht designs (including the one for the Brown family's *Bolero*, seen on page 103), he spoke the language of falling in love. "Olin's lines," he said, "reach right into your heart."

Felt this way, the vessel may be graceful, yes, and even lovely. But she is more than that—she is something to be *used* and not just looked at. A sailboat is not a vase of flowers sitting prettily on a table. She is an active, functioning being whose calling is to work her way through elements that can be friendly but are sometimes harsh and occasionally cruel. Olin Stephens has said that he decided on a boat's looks by envisioning how she would handle heavy weather: "Thinking of appearance, I try to picture a boat running down and dirty. Would it still look right?" Stanley's father, Morris Rosenfeld (who took more than half of the photographs here) made the same point slightly differently. "Every sailorman knows that a ship's beauty is the beauty of utility," he wrote, adding, "the most beautiful hull is the one that will best meet the sea, the most beautiful masts and sails are those which will drive a ship fastest." In other words, anybody considering aesthetics of boats only when they are at anchor is missing much of the point, which is why none of the photographs here shows a boat at rest.

When sailors consider the mix between looks and utility, they lean on a few technical terms. "Seaworthy" can be a polite way to describe an awkward, slow, and boxy boat, though fast boats can be seaworthy, too. "Seakindly" is more precise; seakindly boats get through waves without heaving and throwing mountains of spray. A third, more general, term for an appearance that promises good behavior in bad times is "handsome," as in "handsome is as handsome does."

While I like and use those three terms, I have come to prefer a fourth that is often used among nonsailors who like boats. That word is "sleek." In its best sense it indicates all three qualities—handsome and seakindly and seaworthy (and fast and graceful, too). According to the *Oxford English Dictionary*, "sleek" is derived from a Middle English word *slike* ("slick") and has long meant "smooth," "unruffled," or "tranquil." The sea, of course, is very rarely unruffled and sometimes decidedly untranquil. While some boats perform better in light winds than in heavy, or vice versa, a well-sailed sleek boat will maintain an unruffled demeanor regardless of the conditions.

Sleekness is exemplified by these photographs, which prove that good yacht photographers and good yacht designers are artists with a mutual appreciation for the sea. One art meets another here, for as vigorously as people argue that yacht design and photography are sciences, artistry remains their dominant feature. The boat must fit the water, and the boat and water must fit the viewfinder. It takes a good boat to be sleek, and a good photograph to capture it, and there is more than one type of the first and more than one style of the second.

The dynamic marriage between yacht design and yacht photography is a unifying theme of this selection of photographs culled from thousands in the Rosenfeld Collection. Many of these pictures are published here for the first time, most of them are printed from scans of original vintage prints, and some are shown at their actual size. These images of boats ranging from 15 to 186 feet in length were taken between 1890 and 1955 by Arthur F. Aldridge, Charles E. Bolles, James Burton, or Morris Rosenfeld or his sons. A common element among these photographs is a boat sailing low in the water, her sails textured and multihued with backlighting, and her bow thrusting toward or away from the camera. That is not to say that these rules always apply or that one photograph looks like another. These photographers were too good and too ambitious not to experiment. Morris Rosenfeld's extraordinary shot of the racing schooners *Irolita* and *Elena* bow to bow (page 41) violates all those rules, and nobody can quarrel with the result.

Neither is it correct to say that these boats look alike, as though this were just another set of old black-and-white boat photographs. For a telling example of the range of styles, look at the three images on pages 32 and 33 and the frontispiece, all taken in 1901 or 1903 of immense single-masted Big Class racing sloops built for the America's Cup.

"The America's Cup, after all, is a synonym of things brave and big and famous." That injunction by a yachting writer is an apt caption for these three images, each with its own mood. Although the three photographers were looking at the same or similar boats, and very likely were working with similar equipment and from similar platforms, each presented his subject with a unique vision not only of the boat but of the sea. Bolles's *Columbia*, shot from ahead, is so beautifully proportioned that she might be any size. Burton's *Reliance* is a nautical version of a sledgehammer, suiting the reputation of the largest of all racing sloops. "*Columbia* and *Constitution*" (Aldridge's only picture here and an image that is rarely reproduced) presents a timeless, ominous ocean upon which boats make their way mysteriously.

The variety of interpretation in and novelty of these photographs allow a fresh look at the changing styles in both yacht design and yacht photography. Before discussing the boats themselves, we should take a moment to list the elements of appearance that can make for sleekness.

The bow usually grabs the eye first. It may be nearly vertical, its abruptness softened by hollows in the hull or the curves of a rounded clipper bow, as in *America* (page 37). Or the bow may be spoon-shaped and overhang the water for a great distance, like *Columbia*'s (page 32). A bowsprit may extend far beyond the bow to support the jibs, the sails ahead of the mast. Sheer—the elevation of the boat's sides—is the next crucial element. It usually is highest at the bow to keep heavy water off the deck, and then it dips or even swoops to rise again near the stern. A flat sheer looks convex and makes a boat look hog-backed (as can the color white, which is why the sleekest boats often are painted dark colors). The sheer guides the eye to the stern, which can either balance the bow's shape or be blunt. Aloft, the number and height of the masts vary from boat to boat. Sloops and cutters have one mast, schooners have two or more tall ones (the shortest toward the bow), and yawls and ketches have a tall mast and a shorter one toward the stern. Until the recent development of electric and hydraulic sail-handling gear, larger boats tended to have more masts to allow their sails to be smaller and easier to manage, although the traditional look of the schooner rig is admirable even in small boats. The mainsail is four-sided in the old gaff-headed rig or triangular in the Marconi rig that was introduced in the 1920s, but whatever the rig, every sail is three-dimensional, not flat. Curvature shapes the wind and creates forward drive.

All these factors, and others such as the shape of the hull underwater, are subject to a few standards of which aesthetics is only one. Another is physics: long boats usually sail faster than short ones, and light boats often are faster than heavy ones. A third standard that affects design and, therefore, appearance, but that usually does not receive proper recognition, is the influence of measurement rules that handicap boats for racing and that can cause owners to rebuild their boats and even make them slower in order to take advantage of the rule.

Before the American Civil War, most yachts were little more than polished-up versions of commercial vessels. The best-known example is *America*, built in 1851 along the lines of a New York pilot boat. Later there developed a distinctly American and wonderfully voluptuous style of yacht exemplified here by the curvaceous *Fanny* and *Gracie* (pages 2 and 5). A reaction set in during the 1890s on the heels of new discoveries about racing yacht design and new ways to get around the restrictions of measurement rules. Nathanael Greene Herreshoff in America and George L. Watson and William Fife III in Britain straightened the curves, extended the bows, squared the sterns, lengthened the masts—in sum, launched a new generation of boats whose appearance was sleek in a handsome way rather than the classically beautiful way of the older boats.

This modern functional appearance ruled for many years in big boats and also in the increasing number of small ones as yachting became more democratic. The introduction of the Marconi rig led to another rethinking, with a new efficient, contained, yet in its own way marvelously sleek look that dominated until after the end of the period covered by this book. Good examples are two boats designed by Olin Stephens over a period of almost twenty years, *Dorade* and *Bolero* (pages 70 and 103). Like the architects of most of the boats illustrated here, Stephens carried in his head an ideal shape or template that in his case was defined by balance between the bow and stern. As he explained in his book *Lines*, "I tried to be particular about balance between the ends, and, as far as possible, balance throughout."

The fifty-year evolution to symmetry from voluptuousness was not as fated or straightforward as this thumbnail summary suggests. The round look was not forgotten. John G. Alden's semifisherman schooners, like *Sachem II* (page 48), were a link to commercial seafaring. The astonishing ketch *Ticonderoga* (page 100), with her clipper bow and sweet profile, was a flashback to *Fanny*. And the International One Design (page 101) owed its existence to a man's falling in love with a uniquely graceful stern of the sort that might well have been found on a boat in 1880.

The voluptuous look returned, not in hulls but in sails. Until around 1930, sails were kept relatively small by weak fabrics that could not support much area effectively. A typical racing sloop could fly four or five sails at once—two or three jibs, a gaff-headed mainsail, and a main topsail. A big Herreshoff racing schooner could carry as many as eight sails. That fragmented mass of canvas spilling over the bow and stern may have worn out the sailors, but it challenged photographers who were fascinated by the shadows cast by all those sails. For a brilliant example of the possibilities, look at Morris Rosenfeld's startlingly abstract photograph of *Elena* and *Irolita* on page 41. In the 1920s sail plans were narrowed and simplified as rigs and sail fabrics were strengthened. The Marconi rig eliminated the gaff topsail, the big overlapping genoa jib took the place of all those little jibs, and the buxom parachute spinnaker—one of the best things that ever happened both for sailors and for sailboat photographers—replaced an old combination of small spinnaker and balloon jib. The new simplicity produced a new look. By the mid-1930s a racing sloop was setting only two sails at a time directly over the hull, and cameras were searching for a few deep curves instead of many small shadows.

Many of those changes were made to improve a boat's performance, which is measured in numbers—so many knots of speed, so many degrees sailed closer to the wind. Yet if you were to ask an older yacht designer whether design is primarily an art or a science, he would tell you, as Olin Stephens told me, that it is an art influenced by science.

This is not a surprising answer to come from a man who, while working hard to evaluate boats scientifically in towing tanks and with computers, had three artistic hobbies—painting, music, and architecture. Yet Stephens is hardly alone among the designers of beautiful (or handsome) boats represented in these pages. A. Cary Smith, who drew *Carol* (page 60), was a professional oil painter as well as a professional yacht designer. Of William Gardner, the designer of *Atlantic* (page 57), it was said that "To him the sailing yacht was man's most beautiful creation, and the designing of it the finest of arts." L. Francis Herreshoff, who drew the magnificent *Ticonderoga* (page 100), enjoyed expounding at length and with shock effect on the theory and practice of making yachts better boats by making them lovely. "The beautiful yacht may not be the fastest," he observed, "but like the beautiful woman, she usually is. . . . They seem to have been born under a lucky star which directs their destiny." Although good-looking boats (like good-looking women and men) have been known to come to grief, what is important here is the theory that in the design of sailing yachts, artistry counts in more ways than just in the effort to gather praise and admiration.

That yacht photography, like yacht design, is an art assisted by science is clear in the work of Charles E. Bolles and James Burton, two New York photographers who worked around the turn of the twentieth century, and whose large, superb collections were acquired by another New York artist with a camera, Morris Rosenfeld, after he set up shop on his own in 1910.

It is important to place them in the historical setting. When Bolles and Burton were active, photography was undergoing a revolution that shifted interest away from older, simplistic, clumsy ways of looking at boats. While they took full-frame portraits that superficially resembled the work of older artists, the new images were more subtle and interesting than both the dull, standard-issue ship portrait that served as an official record of a vessel's identification and the popular sail-into-the-sunset tripe that lined the walls of front parlors. Aided by advances in photographic technology—better optics, faster and more sensitive emulsions, and somewhat more portable cameras—the best new photographers successfully resisted being limited by the conventions of showing either all facts or all sentimentality.

Photography was the radically new medium of touching emotions while sending information. By 1899 photography was considered so much a part of sailing that Sir Thomas Lipton, that master of publicity, went to the effort of equipping his first America's Cup challenger, *Shamrock*, with cameras and film and shipping the exposures to Britain to be developed for publication. The independent professional photographers, meanwhile, were experimenting with light, shadow, camera angles, and darkroom techniques to look more deeply into the boat and the moment. That photographs were worth thinking about seriously was fully in the air at the turn from the nineteenth century to the twentieth. Popular magazines were running long essays on photographing the sea and on using new darkroom techniques to print clouds onto an otherwise flat scene. The influential prophet of taking photography out of the studio, Alfred Stieglitz, proclaimed, "Where there is light, one can photograph," and was roaming the streets with small waterproof cameras, taking shadowy photographs of horses and pedestrians. In his frequent, widely distributed writings, Stieglitz laid down a new professional discipline that went beyond the cheap and easy shot taken in a controlled environment. To take pictures with the new cameras, he wrote in an influential essay in 1897, "it is well to choose your subject, regardless of figures, and carefully study the lines and lighting. After having determined upon these," Stieglitz went on, "watch the passing figures and await the moment in which everything is in balance; that is, satisfies your eye." In other words, *think* and *wait* until the right moment before taking the picture.

Such disciplines were observed by Charles E. Bolles, who described his vocation as "artistic photography" and won a gold medal at an international photography congress, and by James Burton, for whom Morris Rosenfeld did darkroom work. After Burton died in 1910, he was eulogized in a way that says much about the new school of yacht photography: "More than most marine photographers, Jim Burton caught the bigness of the sport, and the beauty and sweep of it," wrote Herbert L. Stone, the editor of *Yachting* magazine. "His pictures were, in point of crucial timeliness, unmatched. The sensational instinct was strong in him; he knew just when the fitting time for the snapping of the shutter had arrived—and he never wasted plates." There it is again—that thoughtfulness.

Many years later Stanley Rosenfeld made this point when he said, "We didn't just 'make a photograph.'" Although he acquired modern cameras, Stanley kept the old discipline close to heart, as the photographer Guy Gurney indicated in an account of working near him at the 1995 America's Cup match off San Diego:

> *What struck me was that while I, like the others, was staggering under the weight of three cameras with motor drives, fitted with huge long lenses—300, 500, and 600 mm—Stan was armed with a single, non-motorized 35 mm body with a modest zoom lens. That day I rattled off maybe a dozen rolls of film, and I suppose I got some good images, I don't remember. We photogs sounded like a machine-gun battery every time the cup yachts went near each other. But Stanley worked differently. Every now and then you'd hear a quiet click from his direction, and you'd know he'd made an image. That day he used only one roll of film. Later I spoke with the magazine editor for whom he was shooting, and she told me that every picture on that roll was a winner—sharp, well-exposed, perfectly composed, and a great image. At this point Stanley was seventy-nine years old and getting frail, but still every inch a pro.*

So when Morris Rosenfeld opened his studio in 1910, he was photographing on the shoulders of, if not giants, at least some able professional artists. He had run a portrait studio and found similarities between that work and yacht photography: "Every yacht, I discovered, has its best photographic angle—like every woman's face. And the first approach in taking pictures of a yacht, as in taking pictures of a woman's face, is to study the subject and find out what that angle is." Rosenfeld was still doing it in 1939, when he became obsessed with the play of light on the curves of the vast, deep, new parachute spinnakers. Like the portrait photographer he had been, catching the changing moods on a face—or like Stieglitz photographing clouds, or Monet tracing the vagaries of light on the same haystack—Rosenfeld shot those alluring sails day after day at great cost of time and effort. These extraordinary images, a few of which are shown here on pages 94–96, may be sailing's version of the still life.

Such pictures were possible because the Rosenfelds (unlike Bolles and Burton) enjoyed the freedom of their own private shooting platform. After he went into business for himself, Morris tired of being dependent on official spectator boats, which were slow and unmaneuverable, their decks too high for decent vantage points, and too crowded with competing photographers for him to get a unique shot. So he bought his own small chase boats, all called *Foto*, eventually settling on a twenty-knot runabout that could keep up even with the cup boats and big schooners. While the *Foto*s offered freedom, they also made the physically demanding profession of yacht photography into a contact sport as they careered through rough seas. "I have been knocked down on many occasions while taking pictures at sea," Rosenfeld admitted, adding that there were "many cuts and bruises." The work also bruised relations with *Foto*'s helmsmen—his sons, David, William, and Stanley, all struggling to satisfy their demanding father while coping with sea and wind. Various accounts suggest that Morris and Stanley may have come to blows after Stanley gunned *Foto* to dodge a wave at just the moment his father had his camera focused perfectly on a boat. While that argument may have been fiercer than most, it was part of just another day at an intensely demanding office.

"No other kind of camerawork is more difficult than marine photography," observed a writer familiar with the Rosenfelds' daily grind. That was just as true of the early photographers. The Rosenfelds merely lost their tempers, but Charles E. Bolles's health was so damaged by twenty-five years of long hours on the water that he retired early in 1907 and spent his last years selling real estate in Brooklyn. The fact of the matter is that, as art went, photographing boats was hard work that required concentration, knowledge, patience, and intense, heavy labor.

Burton was probably best prepared for these rigors, thanks to his experience as a combat photographer in the Spanish-American War, where he also spent long days exposed to the elements as he lugged heavy, delicate 8 x 10 cameras, with their tripods and glass plates. Burton was hardly squeamish. He opened an article titled "Adventures of a Yacht Photographer" with this sentence: "The great charm of yacht photography lies in its picturesqueness and its spice and danger." Yet even he was at times intimidated by the struggle to get a good picture, which he called "the very uncertainty of the whole thing." Sometimes the wind died, leaving him baking in the hot sun, desperately searching for reflections to shoot in order to make the long day worthwhile. Often there was salt spray or rain (or both) to soak cameras. In search of the elusive and much-prized low vantage point, which allowed waves to show their true height and shape and dramatized yachts, he liked to go out in stake boats—small vessels without engines that were anchored near race turning marks. Once, Burton's ride home failed to appear, and he was left alone well into the night in a pouring rain.

But there were days when the picture was worth every price. "Lying in wait for a snapshot at a large schooner or a ninety-footer," Burton exuded, "it is a unique and wonderful sensation that one gets as the great, towering clouds of canvas loom above you." As the huge yachts raced by, setting off steep rolling wakes and casting sheets of salt spray, the photographer kept snapping away until forced either to throw himself down into the bilge to keep from being tossed overboard or to cover his equipment. Always, though, there was the sense of awe at the sight of the great vessels that ruled yacht racing in those days when the boats were huge and aristocratic, and photography was a new art: "The delight of every true yacht photographer is a strong breeze. Then the pictures have life in them, and there is an excitement and element of danger present that appeals to everyone who has good, red blood in his veins."

We have been speaking of the fit between the boat and the sea, and the fit between the photographer and the boat herself, with all her awe-inspiring bulk, and her sinuous curves and plays of light and shadow. Here in pictures and text we will try to document these two fits, and these relationships between the sea, the boat, the photographer, and (ultimately) the viewer.

Unknown photographer, Morris Rosenfeld and *Foto*, 1938

Charles Edwin Bolles, *Vigilant* and *Jubilee*, 1893

Visions Transcending
Human Experience

The photograph of *Shamrock IV*'s crew on the previous spread represents yachting's most familiar public image before the 1920s, one of big boats manned by many sturdy professionals under the supervision of a few aristocratic amateurs. As charming as it is, the image is simplistic and inaccurate. The pastime actually was quite diverse, with boats of all sizes sailed by people of many types. And yet this perception is understandable, given how the America's Cup matches stirred up patriotic passion and widespread fascination with spectacular, sleek yachts owned by wealthy, sleek men—like the New York Yacht Club commodore who, it was said, "thought no more of buying a yacht than the average man does of picking up a paper as he passes a newsstand."

A newspaper is a staple of life, however, and not a disposable 130-foot racing yacht. These modern-day Medicis could have chosen many other, less-beautiful things to spend their money on, including cheap, ugly boats from third-rate shipyards. Ordering a superbly built Herreshoff Big Class sloop was the equivalent of tossing several million of today's dollars into the teeth of a gale, so brief was the life of these narrowly specialized boats. The only mementos of those pricey summers of glory were a few trophies and an album of photographs, including many of the ones here. No wonder Nathanael Herreshoff observed, "It is a game for the wealthy, so let them choose the type and size of craft."

These pages prove that many of those choices led to attractive boats. For more information about these yachts and the photographs, consult the descriptions between pages 107 and 118. Here I will say a few words about the working conditions of the two artists who brought them to you—the designer and the photographer.

Looking at these images, I am reminded of the historian Samuel Eliot Morison's observation about the creators of the best clipper ships. Like the architects of medieval Gothic cathedrals, he wrote, those American shipwrights had rare insights into creativity—insights that Morison called "visions transcending human experience, with the power to transmute them into reality." This can also be said of Herreshoff, George L. Watson, William Gardner, and others who drew the lines of the majestic sloops and schooners shown here. They were urged on by creativity, not greed, for few fortunes have been made designing yachts. When A. Cary Smith was asked about a career in yacht design, he advised that happier prospects would be had by a street-corner peanuts salesman.

The designer most closely identified with this period did better than that. Nathanael Greene Herreshoff designed and constructed fourteen of the boats or classes represented here. A lifelong sailor, a nautical experimenter, and a university-educated engineer, in 1878 he joined his equally brilliant, blind brother John Brown Herreshoff in founding the Herreshoff Manufacturing Co. in Bristol, Rhode Island. Out of Bristol came six America's Cup winners, seven racing schooners between 120 and 162 feet, ten important one-design classes, and hundreds of other large and small sail or power vessels. Among the many technical innovations credited in part or whole to Herreshoff are the modern sailboat profile with long overhangs, the turnbuckle for adjusting rigging, and systems of strong, lightweight construction.

Modern in every other way, Herreshoff insisted on designing boats by means of the traditional, tactile craft of sculpting models out of pine instead of drawing plans on sheets of paper or linen. According to his son Francis, he carved the model for the cup defender *Reliance* in a little over two evenings. This anecdote indicates the man's genius and also his ambivalence about his family. Francis found his father wanting in warmth by comparison with his uncle John: "J. B. was human even if N. G. was too busy to be, and a mechanical genius is not meant to be human." Francis's animus may have been heated by a dispute over first principles. His own passion lay with beauty, his father's with performance, which Francis slighted as merely "mechanical." Out of Bristol came *Columbia*, *Irolita*, and other gems, and also many boats that were more handsome in a utilitarian way than as works of art. Yet sleekness ultimately is a measure of a boat's appearance under sail, and there Captain Nat did consistently well.

The owner, designer, and builder each deserve credit for the construction of the yacht. Public awareness of her charms is not their concern. Herreshoff deeply distrusted journalists and photographers, going so far as to hire Pinkerton guards to muscle them off the grounds of his shipyard. On the water, photographers had pretty much a free hand, but their work was not widely available until the late 1890s. That was because the technology did not exist for the mass media to publish photographs until 1897, when high-speed presses first used the halftone printing process. Suddenly, pictures by Bolles, Burton, and other photographers were regularly available in newspapers, in *Harper's Weekly* and other popular magazines, and in the many boating and photography periodicals. This was how the world at large discovered that yachts and their photographs could be works of art.

This broader circulation firmed up their professional standing and financial security, yet photographers were obliged by the pastime's seasonality and economic vagaries to take on other assignments. Charles E. Bolles ran a portrait studio in Brooklyn for many years. James Burton sold photographic equipment and served as a combat, sports, and news photographer. Arthur F. Aldridge worked as a writer and editor. Morris Rosenfeld and his sons took at least as many photographs for industrial clients as they did of yachts. All the same, these photographers between them covered every America's Cup match between

1881 and 1995, plus most New York Yacht Club regattas and any number of other events on the American East Coast and Great Lakes.

The photographers also ran successful businesses producing yacht portraits on demand. Some photographs here must have originated in those scheduled photo sessions. In the 1890s, Bolles's business card carried an offer to photograph sailing or steam yachts under weigh and also to take pictures of cabin interiors. "Duplicates can always be had," he promised, anticipating that proud boat owners might like to give pictures to friends and relatives. Bolles was aggressive in other ways. He protected his creative rights ferociously, copyrighting each image and clearly embossing the words "Bolles *fecit*" (Latin for "Bolles made it") in a large font on every print, a practice that was picked up by other photographers. When one of his pictures ran in a magazine without his permission, Bolles sued the publisher for $50,000—the equivalent of $1 million today. Though he lost on a technicality, he made his point.

A demanding business for Bolles remained one for the Rosenfelds, as I can testify. In the 1950s, just at the end of this book's scope, their chase boat, *Foto*, appeared by appointment in Cold Spring Harbor, Long Island, to take photographs of our club's fleet of Atlantics. Stanley, who I believe was in charge, commanded us to line up and sail by him like so many ducks in a row. My father granted me the privilege of steering our old wooden *Lynx*, still flying musty cotton sails that I can smell to this day.

Years later, as a junior editor at *Yachting* magazine, I watched with fascination as Stanley regularly swept into the office with dozens of fresh new slides under his arm, each frame clearly stamped "Morris Rosenfeld & Sons." Like a card dealer he tossed slides, half a dozen at a time, onto a light box and paused for a reaction from the editor. "That one," and the slide was pushed over to the corner for our further consideration. No response, and the card shark quickly gathered up his beauties and dealt another hand until there were no slides left and, the culling done, he raced off to the next magazine on his list.

This seemed a little ruthless to me then, but the approach became understandable when Stanley later told me what it had been like to work during the Great Depression, when commissions were few. His father carefully photographed the big yachts from all angles and placed the best prints in leather-bound albums, each one customized for an owner. He then sent his young son up to Newport with a stack of albums to peddle. Coming aboard the yacht, Stanley sat with the owner and slowly reviewed the images, one by one, pausing to point out especially fine representations of this yacht's innate beauty. Invariably, he told me, when they reached the back page and he shut the album, the commodore turned to him and said, "Those are very nice photographs, young man. Thank you so much for showing them to me"—leaving Stanley, alas, to return to New York without having made a sale.

Charles Edwin Bolles, *Defender*, 1895

Charles Edwin Bolles, *Defender*, 1895

Charles Edwin Bolles, *Al-Anka*, 1897

Charles Edwin Bolles, *Auraka* and *Idea*, 1897

Charles Edwin Bolles, *Columbia*, 1899

James Burton, *Reliance*, 1903

James Burton, *Columbia* and *Shamrock II*, 1901

James Burton, *Gardenia*, 1906

Charles Edwin Bolles, *America*, circa 1901

Morris Rosenfeld, New York 50s, Starting, 1913

Morris Rosenfeld, New York 50s, Starting, 1913

Morris Rosenfeld, New York 50s, Going for the Start, 1913

Morris Rosenfeld, *Elena* and *Irolita*, 1914

41

Morris Rosenfeld, Sunlight, 1915

43

Morris Rosenfeld, The Afterguard of *Shamrock IV*, 1920

Morris Rosenfeld, *Shamrock IV* Leads *Resolute*, 1920

45

Morris Rosenfeld, *Pintail*, 1923

Morris Rosenfeld, *Halcyon* and *Algol*, 1924

Morris Rosenfeld, *Sachem II*, 1925

Morris Rosenfeld, *Nadji* and *Jeifeen*, 1926

49

Morris Rosenfeld, Interclub Class Start, Larchmont, 1926

(top) Morris Rosenfeld, New York 30s, 1926   (bottom) Morris Rosenfeld, *Walrus*, 1926

Morris Rosenfeld, *Silhouette III*, 1928

Morris Rosenfeld, *Celeritas*, 1928

Morris Rosenfeld, Wee Scot Class, Mark Rounding, 1929

Morris Rosenfeld, Sound Interclubs, 1929

Morris Rosenfeld, *Atlantic*, 1929

Morris Rosenfeld, *Carol*, 1930

Facing the Action

As the exciting and at the same time charming picture on the previous spread shows, yachting was becoming more athletic and democratic, and the photographers (including the Rosenfelds dogging *Typhoon*'s stern) worked hard to get close enough to the action to show it. Equally indicative of the new era is a comparison between the photographs on pages 54 and 57. In the first, twelve little Wee Scots loop a race mark, representing a total of 183 feet of boat length, two dozen boy or girl sailors, and less than $5,000 in total expenditure. Turn to page 57, to the schooner *Atlantic*: 184 feet long, two dozen professional sailors, and upkeep running at least $5,000 a month.

Yes, the America's Cup remained yachting's holy grail, and *Atlantic* and the Big Class sloops, built of gleaming hardwoods and glistening marble, continued to fly the flags of yacht clubs. Yet with every year, the old school became an ever smaller gilded snippet of a far larger pastime. For each 130-footer there were dozens of new, smaller boats. Even the New York Yacht Club, so famous for its luxury yachts, went to the Herreshoffs for one-design classes as small as forty-two feet. With the smaller sailboats came new understandings of sleekness. The fundamental rule had not budged: to best gauge a boat's beauty, see how she performs. As Norman L. Skene wrote in the 1920s in his manual on yacht design, "The design in its entirety should be a frank, vigorous declaration of the use to which the boat is to be put." What changed was the variety of uses to which boats began to be put. That is in part why, in the 1920s, the language of the look of boats acquired two new terms: "wholesome" and "easy."

"Wholesome" was a judgment of extreme trends in yacht design dating back to the 1890s. Seawanhaka Cuppers, *Reliance*, and other highly specialized scow-type racing boats were widely considered to be deficient (even vaguely immoral) because, unlike traditional seagoing boats, they could not safely go out in a hard blow. You can take a wholesome boat out for a sail in a nice, fresh breeze without fear of sinking and pounding into waves so madly that the sailors lose their footing or their lunch. A wholesome boat does not have overlong ends, overlow sheer, and overhigh masts. A wholesome boat, in a word, has heft.

"Easy" was a favorite word of one of the best designers of wholesome boats, John G. Alden of Boston. Criticizing the Herreshoff tradition, he said of his ideal boat that "the generous freeboard and easy sheer, combined with good buoyancy and easy entrance forward, will produce the type of vessel which alone is fit to go to sea." Another way of declaring that a boat should have heft, this rule places the stress on "easy," which indicates an absence of hard turns in the hull. Flowing, easy lines make for a boat with an easy, comfortable motion in a rough sea. Alden's many schooner designs are known as semifisher-men because they share the stocky look of fast New England fishing schooners, like those designed by Alden's mentor, B. B. Crowninshield. Comparing Alden's *Sachem II* (page 48) with the Herreshoff *Typhoon* (page 71), you need not be a yacht designer or even a sailor to appreciate that here are two very different ideas of a proper yacht.

If Alden's boats have probably inspired more affection than the products of any other yacht designer, it is in large part due to their handsome, purposeful, and traditional appearance. But they were also fast, seakindly winners of many of the new ocean races organized after World War I for relatively small boats. When sailboats raced before 1920, it usually was within sight of land, and racing (much less sailing) a boat smaller than sixty feet to Bermuda or Europe was considered daring if not foolish. The average length on deck of the entries in the 1905 race to England (when *Atlantic* set a speed record) was 163 feet; in the 1935 race to Norway, the average boat was only fifty-six feet long from stern to bow.

The ocean-racing dominance of Alden's semifishermen was challenged by a new, very different looking type of boat that lay more in the Herreshoff tradition, although its all-inboard rig was unusually simple. Designed by young Olin Stephens and built by veterans of the old Herreshoff yard, the yawls *Dorade*, *Stormy Weather*, and *Bolero* (pages 70, 84, and 103) were wholesome boats with easy lines, and they were fast as the devil. Traditionalists were at first dubious because the boats lacked some old features, including the gaff-headed schooner rig and the long bowsprit that seamen liked to call "the widow-maker." It is yet another sign of the power of pragmatism that after *Dorade* was launched with a bowsprit, it was removed because, without it, she was easier to sail.

As these new generations of more efficient small boats and offshore racers developed after World War I, a new generation of yacht photographers also made their lives a little easier by shooting from their own chase boats, using new compact equipment.

Morris Rosenfeld was not much of a sailor; his idea of fun on the water was to go fishing. He relied on his sons to drive *Foto*, and they did it well enough, and with such consideration for nearby boats, that race officials usually allowed them to roam freely over the course, even during America's Cup matches. But like all good visual artists, Morris was blessed with a gift for gauging proportions and getting a good read of his subjects. "Every boat has a different motion," he once observed. "No two, even of the same design, sail alike—for no two skippers handle a boat in the same manner." To know that and how to recognize it was like having a key to the bank.

Initially, Rosenfeld, like James Burton and Charles E. Bolles before him, worked with a big 8 x 10 reflex camera that had an awkward tripod and lacked a viewfinder. His peers stayed with that bulky apparatus because they were accustomed to it and liked the results but, when the senior Rosenfeld switched to a smaller, more portable Speed Graphic camera with a viewfinder, he finally was able to see exactly what the camera saw, and that made him more engaged with the picture. "The Graphic gave the photographer a chance to be on his toes," said his son Stanley, "to face the action in front of his camera, and to be more acutely aware of what was happening out there." One proof of the success of the new gear is the wonderfully candid stern-on snapshot that opens this section. Think of the dialogue between photographer and driver as *Foto* rode *Typhoon*'s wake! (Morris, incidentally, tried even smaller 35 mm cameras but, unlike his sons, never used them seriously.)

These pictures are in black and white. Perhaps you have already discovered that fact. Myself, I hardly notice, but I am one of those people who prefer listening to baseball on the radio over watching the game on television. I prefer to decide on my own what color dresses those pretty women are wearing on *Dorade* on that breezy day in 1931, when her young designer sits among them with that happy smile.

It took many years before yacht photographs were usually shot in color. In large part that was due to the long evolution of fast color film, but photographers also preferred black and white because it gave them full control over the image from the moment they chose the film for the day's shoot until processing was over and they had a print. Color slides go to the lab; black-and-white negatives are worked on in-house. "When you're getting into the darkroom, you're starting all over," Stanley Rosenfeld said. Like earlier photographers (including perhaps Burton and Bolles), the Rosenfelds labored in the darkroom to improve images. "If the quality of the sky was uninteresting, we took the time to double-print a cloud in," Stanley explained. "We had a whole library of pictures of different clouds that we had taken from the dock with a low horizon with no trees or houses. We could match the clouds to the weather and the kind of light in the picture. We would print it, all the time shading so the clouds, boat, and water fit."

There's that word again—"fit." Whether accomplished by a photographer working late in the darkroom, or a yacht designer leaning over a drafting table, staring into a computer monitor, or sculpting a model out of pine—however the work is done, there is the passion to look at reality and gauge it against an ideal, and to improve the photograph or boat with a few tiny adjustments so it fits a little better. There we have the common interest of the artists whose work is represented here. As they illustrate the symbiotic relationship between the designer and the photographer, the sailor and the viewer, these photographs force us to evaluate our standards. What do we see? What do we want to see?

Morris Rosenfeld, *Enterprise*, 1930

Morris Rosenfeld, *Shamrock V* and *Enterprise*, 1930

Morris Rosenfeld, *Nadji*, 1930

Morris Rosenfeld, *Anitra*, 1930

Morris Rosenfeld, *Quest*, 1930

Morris Rosenfeld, Sound Interclubs, 1931

Morris Rosenfeld, *Dorade*, 1931

Morris Rosenfeld, *Typhoon*, 1931

Morris Rosenfeld, *Saona III*, 1931

All, Morris Rosenfeld, *Blue Wing*, 1931, *Flapper V*, 1931, *Marita*, 1931
Zaida II, 1931

Morris Rosenfeld, Handicap Class, 1932

Morris Rosenfeld, Sound Interclubs, Start, 1932

Both, Morris Rosenfeld, Victories, 1932

Morris Rosenfeld, *Golliwog*, 1932

Morris Rosenfeld, *Endeavour*, 1934

Morris Rosenfeld, *Rainbow*, 1934

81

Morris Rosenfeld, Wee Scots and a Bullseye, 1933

Morris Rosenfeld, Sound Interclubs, 1936

Morris Rosenfeld, *Edlu* and *Stormy Weather*, 1936

Both, Morris Rosenfeld, *Saraband*, 1936

85

Morris Rosenfeld, *Yankee*, 1937

Morris Rosenfeld, 12 Metre, 1937

Morris Rosenfeld, *Ranger*, 1937

Morris Rosenfeld, *Baruna*, 1938

Morris Rosenfeld, *Persephone*, 1939

Morris Rosenfeld, *Cleopatra's Barge II*, 1939

Morris Rosenfeld, 12 Metres under Spinnaker, 1939

Morris Rosenfeld, 12 Metres under Spinnaker, Rough Water, 1939

Morris Rosenfeld, *Seven Seas*, 1939

Morris Rosenfeld, *Sunbeam*, 1939

Morris Rosenfeld, *Away*, 1947

Morris Rosenfeld, Atlantic 10, 1947

Morris Rosenfeld, *Ticonderoga*, 1949

Morris Rosenfeld, International One Design 2, 1949

Morris Rosenfeld, Lightning 2192, 1954

Morris Rosenfeld, *Bolero*, 1954

Morris Rosenfeld, *Astrild*, 1931

Boat Descriptions

A note on dimensions: Length on deck (also called length overall or LOA) is the distance in feet and inches between the boat's two extreme ends at the stern and bow (the bowsprit, projecting out from the bow, is not measured). Waterline length (LWL) is the boat's greatest length at the water's surface. Beam (BM) and draft (DR) are the boat's greatest width and depth, sail area (SA) is the total area in square feet of the sails (except spinnaker), and displacement (Disp.) is the vessel's weight calculated in long tons of 2,240 pounds. Some of these dimensions may not be available.

page 2, *Fanny*, 1892

Here is the voluptuous style of American yachts built between the Civil War and 1890. Each of *Fanny*'s curves segues gracefully into another. The eye glides from her clipper bow along the deck's swooping sheerline to the petite stern, then up the gently swelling gaff-headed mainsail and topsail above it, and finally down and around the rain-dampened spinnaker. Built in 1874 by D. O. Richmond in Mystic, Connecticut, for Charles H. Mallory, *Fanny* was frequently modified over her long, successful career to meet the demands of ambitious owners and changes in racing measurement rules. Her dimensions in 1892: length on deck 78', waterline length 66', beam 23' 3", draft 6' 9", displacement 46 tons.

page 3, *Elmina*, 1901

The calm is so complete that sailors perch on the schooner's rail and bowsprit, their feet dangling. Her spinnaker and aptly named balloon jib need more wind to iron out their creases. Photographer Charles E. Bolles's eye must have been caught by the flat, triangular shadow cast by all those curves—an irony that also would have appealed to *Elmina*'s artistic designer, A. Cary Smith, a painter who turned to yacht design as a second career. *Elmina* was built in 1901 at the Townsend & Downey yard on Shooters Island, an islet in New York Harbor. Her dimensions: length on deck 99', waterline length 68', beam 20', draft 12'.

page 4, *Canada* and *Zelma*, 1896

Two Canadian boats tune up on Lake Ontario before the first international fresh-water match between the United States and Canada. *Canada* won the trophy, which was later named for her and remains in competition today. *Canada*'s spinnaker, woven from a blend of cotton and silk, would be featherweight except that her crew has accidentally dipped it in the lake. These boats were designed by one of the most artistic of all naval architects, the Scotsman William Fife III. *Canada*'s dimensions: length on deck 54', waterline length 43', beam 11', draft 8', sail area 2,000 square feet. *Zelma*, a champion at Toronto in the early 1890s, was slightly smaller.

page 5, *Gracie*, 1893

Guided by a sailor perched on her bowsprit, the most famous New York racing yacht of the late nineteenth century makes her way to the finish line. The much-altered, black-hulled, clipper-bowed *Gracie* often matched up against *Fanny* in races, surrounded by large bets. "Now I won't go hungry this winter," boasted a *Gracie* crewmember after one victory. Built in 1868 by James E. Smith, of Nyack, New York, to a design by Abraham A. Schank, she had these dimensions when this photograph was taken: length on deck 81', waterline length 72', beam 21' 6", draft 5' 8", sail area 5,400 square feet, displacement 77.6 tons.

page 6, *Constitution* and *Columbia*, 1901

In this haunting photograph, two 130-foot America's Cup sloops drift along, their sails like pyramids above the flat sea. Observing this New York Yacht Club defender elimination race are a three-masted schooner and (under *Constitution*'s boom) J. P. Morgan's steam yacht *Corsair*.

page 12, *Defender*, 1895

"It is a unique and wonderful sensation that one gets as the great, towering clouds of canvas loom above you, James Burton reported. Here, a small stake boat with a photographer balanced on the stern, lies precariously close to *Defender* as she rushes by during the 1895 America's Cup match.

page 21, Morris Rosenfeld and *Foto*, 1938

The Rosenfeld's chase boats, named *Foto*, in combination with smaller cameras permitted a closer view; though still with some physical risk to the photographer. "There were many cuts and bruises," admitted Morris Rosenfeld, here with his Graflex camera.

page 24, *Vigilant* and *Jubilee*, 1893

In its vastness and rough texture, *Vigilant*'s balloon jib might be the face of a granite cliff. The immensity of the Big Class sloops that raced for the America's Cup from 1893 through 1937 can be gauged by the tiny crewman on the bowsprit lifting the sail free of the water. With her designer-builder, Nathanael Greene Herreshoff, at the helm, *Vigilant* won the eighth match for the cup. This was the first of eight cup victories by a boat built at the Herreshoff Manufacturing Co. in Bristol, Rhode Island. Captain Nat was an MIT alumnus with a thorough technical background and a scientist's ruthless approach to his work.

At the end of the nineteenth century, clipper bows were out of date on sailboats. Sleek meant straight edges, skyscraper masts, and lengthy overhangs, with a spoon bow and flat stern extending far over the water. *Vigilant*'s dimensions: length on deck 126' 4", waterline length 85', beam 26', draft 13', sail area 11,672 square feet, displacement 138 tons. *Jubilee*, designed by John B. Paine, had nearly the same dimensions but nowhere near the same speed.

pages 28–29, *Defender*, 1895

The photograph on page 28 at first glance seems to be a classic, elegant yacht portrait, but turns out to be full of action and anxiety as *Defender*'s fifty sailors engage in serious choreography as she approaches a turning mark. The men on the bow and bowsprit—sometimes called "forward fighters" in recognition of their battles with the immense sails—have lowered the balloon jib and hoisted a small jib topsail tied in light twine (called a stop) to keep it under control until the moment for breaking it out. The spinnaker pole, meanwhile, is being swung forward to put that circus-tent-size sail within the grasp of the sailors, who will haul it in. One slip and the sail will go into the water, dragging men with it. Observing from more than seventy feet up is the topmastman, responsible for managing the big topsail. The wind is blowing harder than it seems. Because a high camera angle, like this one from a tug, tends to flatten waves,

the photographers preferred to shoot from small stake boats or powerboats.

Side-on photographs like the one on the right usually make boats look boxy. Not here, thanks to *Defender*'s inherent sleekness and photographer Bolles's quick reaction when an unusually high wave lifted her bow. A Herreshoff creation built of an intricate mix of modern metals, she beat the Earl of Dunraven's *Valkyrie III* in an America's Cup match blackened by charges of cheating. Dimensions: length on deck 123', waterline length 88' 6", beam 23', draft 19', sail area 12,602 square feet, displacement 85 tons.

page 30, *Al-Anka*, 1897
page 31, *Auraka* and *Idea*, 1897

"A fast boat need not of necessity be ugly," it has been said. *Al-Anka*, while sleek, was both fast and ugly. Her look was considered so uncivilized that *Al-Anka*'s owner named her for the Polynesian deity of death. Low-slung, wet, and fragile, she and other pioneer "skimming dishes" were built solely to win the Seawanhaka Cup, established by the Seawanhaka Corinthian Yacht Club, of Oyster Bay, New York, for international races in small boats. The measurement rule established maximum length and sail area, otherwise the designer had pretty much a free hand.

Shooting from a low, small boat, C. E. Bolles catches two more Seawanhaka Cuppers on one of those days when a fresh wind and afternoon sun transform dull water into diamonds. *Idea* is being pushed hard enough to almost leap out of the water, but *Auraka* merely jogs along under a tiny jib and deeply reefed mainsail, her sailors stretched along the rail to keep the boat upright and block water from filling the hull. After a race in which five of nine of these wild boats capsized, a newspaper reporter observed, "It was thus a day of catastrophes."

These boats are the ancestors of the flat-bottomed sailing scows that are popular on small lakes and bays. Dimensions (approximate): length on deck 30', waterline length 17' 6", beam 8' 5", draft 6' (centerboard) or 5' (keel), sail area 500 square feet.

page 32, *Columbia*, 1899

"Nothing so handsome in naval architecture was ever seen," boasted an observer at *Columbia*'s launching. Note the adjective. Successful modern racing boats were *handsome*, not pretty. Yet C. E. Bolles made even this 130-foot racing boat seem almost delicate by taking his picture from slightly ahead, drawing the eye to the slender bow and the gently curved sheer (a perfectly level sheer makes a boat look hump-backed). By including the old schooner in the background, he touched on the theme of the conquest of old technology by the new; this is a nautical version of a Model T leaving a terrified horse and buggy in its dust. The Herreshoff *Columbia* was the first two-time winner of the America's Cup, beating Sir Thomas Lipton's *Shamrock* in 1899 and *Shamrock II* in 1901. Her dimensions: length on deck 131', waterline length 89' 8", beam, 24', draft 19'9", sail area 13,135 square feet, displacement 102 tons.

page 33, *Reliance*, 1903

While C. E. Bolles's *Columbia* is a handsome yacht, James Burton's *Reliance* is a threat. By shooting from slightly astern, Burton emphasized the 1903 America's Cup winner's ruthless force in her blunt stern, hog-backed deck, and sails that might have been cut from steel. She seems to put her rail under not as other boats do, by giving in to the wind's force, but by willfully pressing herself down into the water. This remarkable image expresses the former combat photographer's fascination with danger.

The photo is also true to its subject. A boating writer called *Reliance* an "overgrown ugly brute." After she easily beat Sir Thomas Lipton's *Shamrock III* to win the America's Cup, Lipton's friends tried to console him with compliments about his boat's beauty. "I don't want a beautiful boat," Lipton snapped back. "What I want is a boat to win the cup—a *Reliance*. Give me the homeliest boat that was ever designed, if she is like *Reliance*." The largest racing sloop ever built, *Reliance* stretched more than 200 feet both from top to bottom and from boom end to bowsprit tip. Such vastness could hold a Boeing 767 with room to spare. Her cost was somewhat under $200,000 ($4 million today); her syndicate included a Vanderbilt and a Rockefeller. Her dimensions: length on deck 143' 8", waterline length 89' 8", beam 25' 8", draft 20' 6", sail area 16,159 square feet, displacement approximately 170 tons.

page 34, *Columbia* and *Shamrock II*, 1901

Here is a start in the 1901 America's Cup match. Thanks to her dark green paint, the latest *Shamrock* looks even sleeker than *Columbia*. George L. Watson, Herreshoff's equal as a designer, had gone so far as to test models in a towing tank, and *Shamrock* was at

least theoretically faster than the older *Columbia*. But the Americans had Captain Charlie Barr. In the defender eliminations he had dominated the skipper of a faster boat, Herreshoff's new *Constitution*, and now he took the measure of the challenger. "Handling *Columbia* as a man would a bicycle," reported a journalist, "turning her as on a pivot, he took chances that would have been dangerous in the extreme for the average good skipper." This remains one of the closest matches in America's Cup history; the boats finished one race just two seconds apart. *Shamrock II*'s dimensions: length on deck 137', waterline length 89' 3", beam 24' 6", draft 21' 3", sail area 14,027 square feet, displacement 129 tons.

page 35, *Gardenia*, 1906

A 60-foot sloop barrels along as a professional sailor in white uniform (cap and all) balances precariously on the bowsprit, feeding a jib up the headstay. *Gardenia* will soon fly by, throwing enough spray and waves for James Burton to fear for his cameras. "The great charm of yacht photography," he once observed, "lies in its picturesqueness and its spice and danger." *Gardenia* was designed by William Gardner and built in 1906 at the Wood yard on City Island, New York. One year she won sixteen out of nineteen starts. Dimensions: length on deck 60', waterline length 41', beam 12', draft 8', displacement 16 tons.

page 37, *America*, circa 1901

A national icon at the age of fifty, here is the schooner yacht *America* in her last year under sail. She is somewhat altered from her original piratical appearance. Her masts are now vertical, her sides painted white, yet the famous sharp bow still slices through a wave. Launched in 1851 and boldly named for her country, she sailed to England and won a race and the trophy that her owners established as "perpetually a challenge cup for friendly competition between foreign countries." The America's Cup became the standard for the highest achievement in international yacht racing. *America* was built on Manhattan Island by William H. Brown to a design by George Steers, whose sense of proportion is nicely summarized in his theory that the ideal taper to the bow and stern was "just like the well-formed leg of a woman." *America*'s exact dimensions have been long debated, but here is an approximation: overall length 100', waterline length 90' 4", beam 22' 6", draft 11' 6", sail area 5,263 square feet.

pages 38–39, New York 50s, Starting, 1913

New York 50s are about to start two races. In the photo on the right, the clever leader holds high to squeeze her competitors into each other's broken air. Judging by the gradually smaller bow waves and increasingly upright masts, the tactic is working.

One of the classes of boats of the same design that appeared after 1900 to provide close, relatively inexpensive competition, the 50 was designed and built by Herreshoff for the New York Yacht Club (the number is the waterline length, the best indicator of a boat's size and potential speed). The simple knockabout rig, with no bowsprit to serve as a tightrope for brave sailors, made them easy to handle by mostly amateur crews. The 50s were the most successful of the large classes, and also the most expensive at $17,000—the equivalent of about $300,000 today. Owners included the tycoons J. P. Morgan, Jr., Harry Payne Whitney, and George F. Baker, Jr. Dimensions: length on deck 72', waterline length 50', beam 14' 6", draft 9' 6", displacement 33 tons.

page 40, New York 50s, Going for the Start, 1913

With only a short while to the starting gun, seven New York 50s are making their final run to the buoy (off camera to the left). The dark boat and three others are early, so they sail down at low speed in hopes of finding a hole ahead of the boat in the foreground and the two that are breaking out their big reaching jibs. The one on the far right risks being left behind the pack. Some shouting and perhaps a collision or two lie in the immediate future. The photograph on page 38 shows the same start a couple of minutes later.

page 41, *Elena* and *Irolita*, 1914

Titled "A Hard Fight for a Windward Berth" when first published in 1914, this picture of two Herreshoff schooners is sublime even though, unlike almost all the other images in this book, it violates rules of sailing photography—three of them, in fact. The boats are not backlit; the sun glaring down from over the photographer's right shoulder bleaches shape and texture out of the sails; and we look at them from two viewpoints—from upwind and from a ninety-degree angle—either one of which alone usually produces an awkward, high-sided appearance. Yet the play of light across the sixteen sails is so intricate (try to trace the source of each shadow) that those big and still-sleek hulls seem to anchor the picture against

flying off into abstraction. *Elena* (left, 1911) and *Irolita* (1906) were two of seven steel racing schooners longer than 120 feet that the Herreshoffs built in the early twentieth century before the arrival of the federal income tax. We will see *Irolita* under another name on page 85. *Elena* dimensions: length on deck 126', waterline length 92' 6", beam 24', draft 14' 1", sail area 11,000 square feet, displacement 160 tons. *Irolita* dimensions: length on deck 136' 6", waterline length 96', beam 26' 8", draft, 16' 11", displacement 206 tons.

page 43, Sunlight, 1915

Despite the name Morris Rosenfeld gave this picture, it appears to be less about the sun than about the lure of the sea that Robert Frost identified in his poem "Neither Out Far Nor In Deep":

> *The people along the sand*
> *All turn and look one way.*
> *They turn their back on the land.*
> *They look at the sea all day.*

page 44, The Afterguard of *Shamrock IV*, 1920

Skipper William P. Burton and his mates were the first amateurs to take charge of an America's Cup boat. Their ties, straw hats, and genteel manners make it hard to take them seriously as racing sailors—that is, unless you know that nobody came closer to winning the cup from the New York Yacht Club before the Australians finally took it away in 1983. Note the paucity of mechanical winches for the white-uniformed professional sailors.

page 45, *Shamrock IV* Leads *Resolute*, 1920

Shamrock IV has the lead on another day in the 1920 America's Cup match. It would have been an unfortunate testimonial for ugly boats had she won the cup. "Something like a cross between a tortoise and an armored cruiser" was the writer Alfred F. Loomis's appraisal of *Shamrock IV*. These boats were smaller, less costly, and more seaworthy than the old Big Class. The sweeter *Resolute*, looking like a big New York 50, was Herreshoff's fifth cup winner and had these dimensions: length on deck 110' 5", waterline length 75', beam 22' 8", draft 13' 8", sail area 10,459 square feet, displacement 108 tons. *Shamrock IV*, designed by Charles E. Nicholson and built by Camper and Nicholsons: length on deck 106' 8", waterline length 75' 6", beam 21' 1", draft 13' 10", sail area 8,775 square feet, displacement 106 tons.

page 46, *Pintail*, 1923

The very opposite of the Big Class America's Cup boats in appearance and price, *Pintail* and the other New York 30s may have looked a little stubby, but they were easy to sail by a crew of amateurs, strongly constructed, and stable enough to carry on through a hard chance without reefing. Nat Herreshoff, no sentimentalist or braggart, predicted they would be "mighty good boats." Eighteen 30s were built in 1905 for members of the New York Yacht Club at a cost of $4,000 each, fully outfitted with sails, anchors, and even china for their small galleys below. Many were still sailing decades later. In the late 1970s *Pintail* made a transatlantic cruise to Norway. Her age caught up with her on the return voyage, however, when she opened up and sank. Dimensions: length on deck 43' 6", waterline length 30', beam 8' 9", draft 6' 4".

page 47, *Halcyon* and *Algol*, 1924

The success of sloops and cutters did not kill off the traditional schooner rig, with its short mast forward and taller one aft. *Halcyon* and *Algol* were two of the popular Sound Schooners that first appeared in 1912. Designed by B. B. Crowninshield of Boston and built by Rice Brothers in East Boothbay, Maine, they were only forty feet on deck. Today that is a decent size, but back then it was a compact package thanks to typically narrow beam and a full inventory of frames, deck beams, and other space-consuming structural members. The Sound Schooner seemed so small that the nickname "Schoonerette" was invented for it by people familiar with boats like *Irolita* and the commercial fishermen that Crowninshield also designed. But the Sound Schooner had its fans. Two were the yacht designers Olin and Rod Stephens, who as teenagers in the 1920s sailed and raced the family boat *Alicia* long and hard. "The things that made her fun were related to her combination of Spartan accommodations, narrow beam, and light displacement," Olin wrote of *Alicia* in his autobiography. "Her general character made her a great boat for a crew of boys rather than a family." He and Rod themselves produced a large number of sleek boats, some of which will grace later pages (for example, page 84). Dimensions: length on deck 40' 11", waterline length 30', beam 7' 11", draft 6' 3", sail area 780 square feet.

page 48, *Sachem II*, 1925

Someone once said of an Alden schooner like *Sachem* that she "looked so warm and friendly we thought of her as alive." The twentieth century's preeminent schooner designer, John G. Alden, developed a style he called "semifisherman" because of its husky, seakindly shape. As *Sachem II* proves, these were hardly crude floating boxes. Neither were they slow. The first four boats in the 1932 race to Bermuda were Alden schooners (the winner was the designer's own *Malabar X*). *Sachem II* here flies a large reaching sail that was unique to schooners and was called, inexplicably, the gollywobbler. She was built at the Pendleton yard in Wiscasset, Maine, of wood (of course). Her dimensions: length on deck 59' 5", waterline length 42', beam 13' 6", draft 8' 2", sail area 1,765 square feet.

page 49, *Nadji* and *Jeifeen*, 1926

Here is the hard-edged modern rig that came of age in the 1920s. Called "jib-headed," "Bermudian," or "Marconi" (the last because it seemed as tall as a radio antenna), it puts sail area up high, where there is more wind, in a triangular configuration on a tall mast held aloft by strong steel wire rigging. The rig is handier and more powerful than the old, squat, gaff-headed arrangement, with its mess of rigging. Marconi-rigged staysail schooners flew several sizes and combinations of sails between the masts, depending on conditions. *Nadji* and *Jeifeen* were Seawanhaka Schooners designed by Cox & Stevens and named for the same club that thirty years earlier stimulated the very different skimming dishes that raced for the Seawanhaka Cup (pages 30–31). Dimensions: length on deck 58' 6", waterline length 38', beam 12', draft 7' 9", sail area 1,413 square feet, displacement 20 tons.

page 50, Interclub Class Start, Larchmont, 1926

As these Interclubs jockeying for position at a stake boat make clear, in the 1920s yachting was no longer what William U. Swan characterized as "the exclusive hobby of a comparatively small number of tremendously wealthy men, willing and able to employ professional captains and professional crews." (The only wrong note in that statement is the apparent disregard of the large number of women sailors.) In 1926, for $2,400, Long Island Sound sailors could buy a new Sound Interclub designed by Charles D. Mower, of whom it was said, "He never designed a slow boat or a homely one." The builder was the Nevins yard, on City Island, New York. Dimensions: length on deck 28' 9", waterline length 19', beam 7' 6", draft 4' 6", sail area 425 square feet.

page 51, (top) New York 30s and (bottom) *Walrus*, 1926

The New York 30s in a strong breeze (under full sail, as usual) illustrate an observation about "that Herreshoff characteristic of passing unperturbed through agitated waters." Below, on a similar day, is the little Crowninshield schooner *Walrus*, the percentage sign on her mainsail indicating that she is racing in a handicap division against boats of different designs. Built by James B. Graves, in Marblehead, Massachusetts, *Walrus* had these dimensions: length on deck 36', waterline length 28', beam 7' 10", draft 5' 4".

page 52, *Silhouette III*, 1928

The close-winded *Silhouette III* was one of eight one-design International 8 Metres designed to the International Rule by the American naval architect W. Starling Burgess and built in 1928 by Abeking & Rasmussen, a German shipyard. In those heady days of an economic boom, the same team also found American buyers for fleets of one-designs in the smaller Atlantic class and larger International 10 and 12 Metre classes. The International Rule defined a boat's size within certain tolerances, depending on the class, and normally permitted small variations in design. By introducing the one-design concept to standardize his boats, Burgess kept costs low. Dimensions: length on deck 48' 6", waterline length 30', beam 8' 9", draft 6' 6", sail area 864 square feet.

page 53, *Celeritas*, 1928

A yacht club looking to build a reputation found it hard to resist an opportunity to adapt a class of large racing yachts. In 1917 members of the Larchmont Yacht Club, on western Long Island Sound near New York City, acquired six Larchmont O Boats. "O" was a rating category that accommodated boats of this size. Originally gaff-headed, they were converted to the new Marconi rig that *Celeritas* flies here in a handy knockabout rig with a jib and a jib topsail. The designer was William Gardner, "by whom," it was once written, "no worthless boat was ever designed." Dimensions: length on deck 59' 10", waterline length 38' 8", beam 12', draft 7' 9", sail area 1,704 square feet, displacement 16 tons.

page 54, Wee Scot Class, Mark Rounding, 1929

Wee Scots swarm around a mark in a race. The smallest boat in this book, the Wee Scot was sailed by youngsters in yacht club junior sailing programs. Originally priced at $350, they were extremely popular. Almost four hundred were built; some are still sailing in Maine. Thomas R. Scott designed them in 1922 and they were built in a boatyard in Rye, New York. Dimensions: overall length 15' 3", waterline length 11' 3", beam 5' 3", draft 3'.

page 55, Sound Interclubs, 1929

The economy is still good in the summer of 1929 as Sound Interclubs make their way down the race course. The Great Depression would force many people back ashore, while at the same time driving down the cost of new boats.

page 57, *Atlantic*, 1929

Here doing at least 15 knots, the 185-foot three-masted schooner *Atlantic* holds the oldest speed record in sailing: the fastest time in a scheduled race from New York to the English Channel. She covered the nearly 3,000 miles in twelve days, four hours, one minute in the 1905 transatlantic race. While a few other boats have done the course faster, all have awaited optimum weather instead of starting a scheduled race. *Atlantic* was commanded on her great run by the hard-driving Charlie Barr, who had won the last three America's Cup matches in *Columbia* and *Reliance*. Asked how he won, Barr said, "It amounts to this: I've got the best yacht afloat." That yacht's designer was William Gardner, one of the leading designers of the period 1890–1930. He had a thorough technical training and produced boats and ships of most types, including commercial steamships and two very different sailboats that are icons in the history of yachting: the 22-foot Star Class one-design, and this great schooner. Built of steel in 1903 at the same yard on Shooters Island where *Elmina* came to life, *Atlantic* raced across the Atlantic another two times and remained active until the 1950s. She was finally broken up in her seventy-third year. The largest boat in this book, *Atlantic* had these dimensions: length on deck 184', waterline length 134', beam 29' 6", draft 17' 6", sail area 18,000 square feet, displacement 206 tons.

page 60, *Carol*, 1930

The schooner *Carol*, twenty-six years of age, reaches fast with a proverbial bone in her teeth, her seven sails pulling like dray horses and the U.S. yacht ensign at its traditional place of honor at the peak of the mainsail gaff. Her designer, A. Cary Smith, was an artist and visionary at both the easel, where he painted portraits of yachts, and at the drafting table, where his designs included the sloop that won the 1881 America's Cup match. He had few illusions about his calling. Asked by a youngster about the prospects of a career in yacht design, he warned, "My boy, you had better get a job on a peanut stand, it will pay you better in the end." Designers of luxury yachts and one-design classes did a little better than that, as did Smith himself once he started designing passenger steamboats. *Carol*, originally *Iris*, was built of steel at the Lawley yard in Boston in 1904 and had these dimensions: length on deck 102' 6", waterline length 71', beam 21' 2", draft 11', sail area 5,533 square feet, displacement 84 tons.

pages 64–65, *Shamrock V* and *Enterprise*, 1930

The J-Class sloops that raced for the America's Cup in the 1930s were almost as long as *Columbia*, *Reliance*, and the other Big Class racers, and often faster, too, despite having half their sail area: the Marconi rig was that efficient. The crews were smaller, too, with thirty instead of fifty or more sailors. In the photo on page 64, if the 1930 cup defender *Enterprise* looks dangerously understaffed, it is because half her crew, called "the black gang," is at work in the bowels of this sailing machine. She was designed by W. Starling Burgess, who as a pioneer aviator knew about saving weight and cutting windage. That is a lifeboat on the stern; more than one Big Class sailor drowned after falling overboard from the unguarded decks.

In the image on the right, *Enterprise*, as usual, leads the last of five challengers sent over by the ever hopeful and much loved Sir Thomas Lipton. The end result in 1930 left even the winner's hard-boiled skipper in a state of despair. "To win the America's Cup is glory enough for any yachtsman, but why should we be verging on the disconsolate?" Harold Vanderbilt wrote as *Enterprise* finished the last race. These boats were in the J Class under the Universal Rule. *Shamrock* is still sailing, while *Enterprise* was scrapped soon after her win. Built of metals at the Herreshoff yard (years after old Nat's retirement), *Enterprise* had these dimensions: length on deck 120', waterline length 80', beam 22' 2", draft 14' 6", sail area 7,583 square feet, displacement 127 tons. *Shamrock V* was designed by Charles E. Nicholson and built (mostly of wood) by Camper and Nicholsons. Dimensions: length on deck 119' 10", waterline length 81', beam 19' 8", draft 14' 8", sail area 7,540 square feet, displacement 134 tons.

page 66, *Nadji*, 1930

A schooner only comes fully alive on a beam reach when—as *Nadji* proves on this windy day—the sheets are freed and the vessel is given her head. A 59-foot Seawanhaka Schooner, *Nadji* is shown on page 49 sailing less rapidly. The low camera angle, which highlighted the sea's roughness and the mixed joys and risks of sailing in hard winds, was a Rosenfeld specialty made possible by the family's small chase boats.

page 67, *Anitra*, 1930

The International 12 Metre *Anitra* rolls along behind a groundswell with her new-fangled genoa jib pulling hard. She was one of six one-design 12s designed by W. Starling Burgess and built in Germany for American customers in 1928. Constructed to an exceptionally high standard, 12s have had long lives. After bouncing around for many years from New England to California to Florida, *Anitra* is today in a charter fleet at Newport, Rhode Island. Dimensions: length on deck 69' 4", waterline length 43', beam 12' 6", draft 8' 6", sail area 1,970 square feet, displacement 24 tons.

page 68, *Quest*, 1930

Quest takes a roll to windward under thunderheads as the foredeck crew strains to hoist the last inches of spinnaker halyard. An International 8 Metre from the Royal Canadian Yacht Club in Toronto, she raced the Rochester (New York) Yacht Club's *Thisbe* in the seventh match for the Canada's Cup (see page 4). *Thisbe* won a thrilling match watched by thousands of spectators on Lake Ontario. The great Scots designer William Fife III designed *Quest*, whose approximate dimensions were: length on deck 48', waterline length 30', beam 8' 9", draft 6' 6", sail area 864 square feet.

page 69, Sound Interclubs, 1931

Few people raced the 8 Metres, while hundreds raced the small one-design keelboat classes that sprouted in the 1920s. Here a large fleet of Interclubs gets off the starting line in a moderate breeze. The confused sea has left number 26 looking very unsleek and almost dead in her tracks.

page 70, *Dorade*, 1931

This boat might at first seem unimportant, what with those men in shirts and ties and the women in dresses, yet *Dorade* was the most revolutionary yacht of her day, and the beaming young man at her helm, twenty-three-year-old Olin Stephens, was becoming the successor to Nat Herreshoff and John Alden as the leading yacht design innovator. Behind him is his younger brother, Rod, already acknowledged as a master of modern rigging and construction. Just a few years ago they were boys ranging the Maine coast in an old Schoonerette (see page 47). Soon they will race *Dorade* to England and win by two days. This photograph shows *Dorade* both a little tippy due to her extreme narrow beam, and also very handsome, with her near-symmetrical bow and stern. "I tried to be particular about balance between the ends, and as far as possible, balance throughout," wrote Olin, for whom yacht design was first an art and then a science. *Dorade* was designed by Sparkman & Stephens and built on City Island, New York, at the Minneford yard by craftsmen who had worked at the old Herreshoff yard. Dimensions: length on deck 52', waterline length 37' 3", beam 10' 3", draft 7' 8", sail area 1,150 square feet, displacement 17 tons.

page 71, *Typhoon*, 1931

In this unusual stern-on view, the New York 40 *Typhoon* works her way upwind on a perfect breezy day, but not so seriously that her crew won't give the cameraman a smile. The photograph is full of technical interest for sailors as well as for marine photographers. In his chase boat, *Foto*, Morris Rosenfeld once got so close to a racing boat that the helmsman invited him to step aboard. The New York 40 was designed and built by the Herreshoff Manufacturing Co. in 1916. Dimensions: length on deck 59', waterline length 40', beam 14' 3", draft 8', displacement 22 tons.

page 72, *Saona III*, 1931

One of John Alden's racier-looking boats, very different from his semifisherman schooners, *Saona* was built in 1915 at the Hodgdon Brothers yard in East Boothbay, Maine. The towering Marconi mainsail must have been added subsequently. Dimensions: length on deck 72', waterline length 50' 4", beam 15' 6", draft 9' 10".

page 73, *Blue Wing, Flapper V, Marita, Zaida II*

Any of these four boats would have been encountered during a weekend afternoon sail on Long Island Sound in the 1930s. Starting at the upper left, we have the popular Atlantic and Victory one-designs. Then come two lovely Alden semifisherman schooners, shown here flying gollywobblers on easy reaches—the 58-foot *Marita* and the 52-foot *Zaida II*, owned by the sailmaker George Ratsey. Both schooners seem too pretty and comfortable to sail as fast as they did. According to one authority, *Zaida II*'s racing record was "quite out of proportion to what you would have expected from glancing at her rather round lines."

page 75, Handicap Class, 1932

Her white sails and deck framed by the black squall toward which she is rapidly sailing, a small cruising boat of about 30 feet works her way to windward during a race. Undoubtedly, her crew is getting anxious.

page 76, Sound Interclubs, Start, 1932

The "V" running down the middle of this photograph of Sound Interclubs will be familiar to both sailors and artists, though they call it by different names. To a sailor it is one of the divisions that define life afloat: a boat is either sailing upwind or sailing downwind, either becalmed or in wind, or (in this case) either climbing up the face of a wave or sliding down into its trough. An artist might call this "V" an element pulling the eye into a well-composed picture. As Stanley Rosenfeld said, "If you look at our photographs, the eye is happy to move around and doesn't get caught off in some corner and stay there. When you look at a photograph, your eye is drawn to a significant place, but then it has to keep moving around the picture. If it doesn't move, that's what I call a hole. You don't want a hole."

page 77, Victories, 1932

The Victory exemplified the formula for success: a hull with no extremes, a large rudder, a small cabin for overnight sailing (here under a flush deck), and a rig handy enough for a crew of three, like the one on the left. Built in 1920 as one of the first Marconi-rigged one-designs, the class was a patriotic exercise. The name honored the victory over Germany in the Great War, and boats were called *Ace*, *Spad*, *A.E.F.*, *Black Jack* (General Pershing's nickname), and similar names. The Victory was designed by William Gardner, who also drew the lines of the great three-master *Atlantic* (page 57). Dimensions: length on deck 31' 6", waterline length 20' 10", beam 7', draft 4' 10", sail area 433 square feet, displacement 2.6 tons.

page 79, *Golliwog*, 1932

The first major innovation after the Marconi rig, the parachute spinnaker did the double duty of the old single-luff spinnaker and balloon jib (see pages 4–5), meanwhile challenging sailors and fascinating photographers no end. The boat in there somewhere is a small Arthur E. Payne–designed cutter built at the Nevins yard in 1930. Because she was owned by a sailmaker, Ernest A. Ratsey, she was a floating laboratory for the new go-fast gear. Dimensions: length on deck 31' 6", waterline length 29' 6", beam 10', draft 5', sail area (without spinnaker) 800 square feet.

page 80, *Endeavour*, 1934

Another new idea in spinnakers was the so-called "Annie Oakley" with vents. It did not succeed. This one is flying on the most beautiful J Class America's Cup yacht, which old Nat Herreshoff called "a perfect boat." Owned and sailed by T. O. M. Sopwith and designed by Charles E. Nicholson, *Endeavour* easily won the first two races of the 1934 match and seemed destined to take it all—until she was undone by her skipper's mistakes, her amateur crew's sailhandling errors, and the cunning of Harold Vanderbilt on the defender *Rainbow*. Like *Shamrock V*, *Endeavour* has undergone a multimillion dollar refit, is regularly sailing, and awing onlookers. Dimensions: length on deck 129' 8", waterline length 84', beam 22', draft 15', sail area 7,561 square feet, displacement 142 tons.

page 81, *Rainbow*, 1934

As her crew runs onto her exceptionally sharp bow to change jibs, *Rainbow* reaches toward the next mark of the course. Even in this light wind she heels enough to dramatically extend her sailing length and, therefore, her potential speed. She barely won the 1934 defender eliminations and came very close to losing the America's Cup altogether to the faster *Endeavour*. Designed by W. Starling Burgess, *Rainbow* was the last cup boat built at the Herreshoff yard. Dimensions: length on deck 127' 8", waterline length 82', beam 21', draft 15', sail area 7,535 square feet, displacement 141 tons.

page 82, Wee Scots and a Bullseye, 1933

A horde of junior sailors inches—and in one case bangs—their way down the last bit of a run in a near calm. If the crew of number 4 were not so preoccupied with catching the last breath of air, they would be counting their blessings that they have reached the buoy in clear air with only one other boat to worry about.

page 83, Sound Interclubs, 1936

With the wind direction just far enough aft to carry parachute spinnakers, two Interclubs blast down a reach on the edge of control, their hulls riding their bow waves. The trailing boat steers above the course in hopes of getting the leader to make a mistake and wipe out. This is a desperate, delicate balancing act for all concerned—even the photographer as *Foto* (her wake just visible in the lower left-hand corner) races ahead to hold the camera angle. Sailors always trusted the Rosenfelds to stay out of their way.

page 84, *Edlu* and *Stormy Weather*, 1936

"*Stormy Weather* possessed a flair exhibited by few boats, an attribute always hard to define but universally recognized." So wrote her designer, Olin Stephens. She and her close cousin beat to windward, *Edlu* under the old double-headsail rig using two relatively small jibs and *Stormy Weather* flying one of the new big overlapping genoa jibs (called that because the first one was used in a race off Genoa, Italy). The backlighting enhances their power, grace, and symmetry. A modern-day yacht designer, Robert Perry, has commented, "I look at the hot boats of today and I look at *Stormy Weather* and I wonder if the big increase in boat speed is enough to offset the loss in aesthetics." The two yawls were designed by

Sparkman & Stephens and built by Nevins in 1934. *Edlu* won the 1934 Bermuda Race, *Stormy Weather* the 1935 transatlantic race to Norway. In 2001 *Stormy Weather* was thoroughly restored in Italy. *Stormy Weather's* dimensions: length on deck 53' 11", waterline length 39' 9", beam 12' 6", draft 7' 10", sail area 1,302 square feet, displacement 18 tons.

page 85, *Saraband*, 1936

Taken the same year as the photographs of the modern yawls on page 94 is this sequence of the 1906 Herreshoff 120-foot schooner *Saraband* (formerly *Irolita*, shown on page 41) roaring through a shining sea on an afternoon sail. At her helm is her owner, John Nicholas Brown, who named all his boats for dances. Two years after these wonderful images were made, *Saraband* was so badly damaged by a hurricane that Brown declined to make repairs. The old era was ending all too quickly.

page 86, *Yankee*, 1937

By now our eyes should be fully accustomed to the Big Class yachts that have been sailing for the America's Cup since 1893, but somehow they always find a way to astonish us. Here, in their final America's Cup summer, the Boston boat *Yankee* slides downwind under her parachute spinnaker. Although she never sailed for the America's Cup, *Yankee* was consistently one of the top Js through the class's short lifespan in America and was especially strong when the wind came up. In the non-cup year of 1935, she took part in a low-key race to England against the old three-masted record-holder *Atlantic* (page 56) and then spent the summer successfully racing English Js. Like almost all the other J boats, *Yankee* was broken up at the beginning of World War II, and her remnants were sold for scrap, the proceeds in her case going to an English charity hospital. Designed by Frank C. Paine, *Yankee* had these dimensions when she was built by Lawley in 1930: length on deck 124', waterline length 83', beam 22' 6", draft 14' 10", sail area 7,288 square feet, displacement 148 tons.

page 87, 12 Metre, 1937

With the Js fading quickly from the scene, a big racing boat of the late 1930s was a 12 Metre, which a generation earlier would have been considered a small boat indeed at 65 feet, with a crew of less than ten to manage sails that, alongside a J boat's, look like handkerchiefs. After more than twenty years, the America's Cup would return to competition in 1958 in these boats.

page 89, *Ranger*, 1937

Inspired by this spectacular photograph of the last of the Big Class yachts, Harold Vanderbilt wrote, "With outstretched wings, white as snow, they are flying towards us in formation. *Ranger*, the fastest all-around sailing vessel that has ever been built, heads the cavalcade. Her four older sisters follow in her train. Soaring, a fresh breeze fills the world's largest sail. Presently, their season's work o'er, they will pass by in review. As they have come out of the distance, so shall they go into the distance. The fair wind, their never weary white wings, carry them on—on the wind's highway, 'homeward bound for orders'—on, to destiny." Racing on the New York Yacht Club Cruise, these five J Class sloops are (left to right) *Yankee*, *Endeavour II*, *Endeavour I*, *Rainbow*, and *Ranger*, winner of the 1937 America's Cup match. Only *Endeavour I* survived the wrecker to sail after World War II. Co-designed by W. Starling Burgess and Olin Stephens, and built at the Bath Iron Works, in Maine, *Ranger* had these dimensions: length on deck 135' 2", waterline length 87', beam 21', draft 15', sail area 7,950 square feet, displacement 175 tons.

page 90, *Baruna*, 1938

The tiny mizzenmast in the yawl rig can help a boat's looks but not her speed, except on a reach, when a lightweight mizzen staysail can be flown. Here it helps *Baruna* plow a deep furrow. Commenting on *Baruna* in the context of today's faster, harder-to-handle, more uncomfortable boats, Olin Stephens asked this rhetorical question: "Why do we have less pleasure as we learn more and more?" "The Big Black B" (as *Baruna* was called in her home port of Cold Spring Harbor, New York) was a Sparkman & Stephens yawl designed to the measurement rule's maximum length. Built at the Quincy Adams yard in Massachusetts, *Baruna* had a few dimensions like the old New York 50s: length on deck 72', waterline length 50', beam 14' 8", draft 9' 2", sail area 2,342 square feet.

page 91, *Persephone*, 1939

Leaving an admirably flat wake as she reaches fast, the ketch *Persephone* was designed by L. Francis Herreshoff, a son of Nat. The boats of L. Francis always had at least one unusual feature. Many were double-ended, with the stern as pointed as the bow. *Persephone* had a more typical stern but was flush-decked, with no cabin visible. When criticized for the low main cabin he designed for the ketch *Ticonderoga* (page 100), L. Francis complained, "It didn't have full head room because it's not a goddam dance hall." *Persephone* was built in 1937 at the Butt Brothers yard in Saugus, Massachusetts. Dimensions: length on deck 55', waterline length 40', beam 12' 8", draft 8'.

page 93, *Cleopatra's Barge II*, 1939

Because history's first luxury yacht is said to be the vessel in which Queen Cleopatra of Egypt was conveyed to meet Mark Antony in 42 B.C., the odd name "Cleopatra's Barge" has sometimes been applied to later pleasure boats. One was America's first large yacht, a strange multicolored vessel that sailed out of Salem, Massachusetts, in 1816 under the command of George Crowninshield, a rotund little man smitten by the idea of meeting, and perhaps rescuing, Napoleon Bonaparte. *Cleopatra's Barge* returned to Salem with some Napoleonic artifacts, including a pair of his boots, now on display in the Peabody Essex Museum. Over a century later, another Crowninshield, Francis, bought a beautiful big Herreshoff schooner similar in looks to *Saraband* and *Elena*, renamed her *Cleopatra's Barge II*, and sailed her on New York Yacht Club cruises. Dimensions: length on deck 109', waterline length 80', beam 23' 9", draft 14' 10".

page 94, 12 Metres under Spinnaker, 1939
page 95, 12 Metres under Spinnaker, rough water, 1939
page 96, *Seven Seas*, 1939

Voluptuous curves came back in style with the invention of the parachute spinnaker, which is seen here on several 12 Metres racing in the last season of serious American sailing before the European (soon to be world) war interfered. Everybody finds these shapes fascinating; the Rosenfelds could perpetuate them. They closely chased the 12s in several races, Morris behind the camera and his son Stanley at the helm of their chase boat, *Foto*. Stanley wrote of these long days in his book *A Century Under Sail*: "To get the sense of sweep and the complementary curves in the sails to harmonize, we had to be precise in our timing, to be both in the right camera position and not to be in the wrong place for our wake. I was at the helm and would move into position, swing the bow, slow down, synchronizing our movements so that I

could say, 'Ready, Dad, ready—shoot.'" These photographs, and the effort it took to take them, make one skeptical of Morris Rosenfeld's claim that he was uninterested in artistic effect. 12 Metre approximate dimensions: length on deck 70', waterline length 45', beam 11' 10", draft 8' 11", sail area 1,850 square feet, displacement 25 tons.

page 97, *Sunbeam*, 1939

A reminder of the curves of the traditional look is provided by this Alden semifisherman schooner of 1922—still with a gaff-headed foresail seventeen years later. The sailor happily seated upon her long bowsprit is very likely not thinking about the theory of spheres and the difficulty of catching them in the right light. Dimensions: length on deck 60', waterline length 43' 6", beam 13' 6", draft 8', sail area 1,780 square feet, displacement 22 tons.

page 98, *Away*, 1947

A New York 32 works her way upwind in deep water as the helmsman steadies her tiller against a hard tug of weather helm. Once she reaches her destination, somewhere beyond this big swell and over the far horizon, the crew will lift the dinghy off the cabin roof and paddle ashore to see the sights. The latest of the New York Yacht Club one-designs, the 32s were designed by Sparkman & Stephens and built at the Nevins yard in 1936. Dimensions: length on deck 45' 4", waterline length 32', beam 10' 7", draft 6' 6", sail area 990 square feet, displacement 11 tons.

page 99, Atlantic 10, 1947

Ninety-nine Atlantics were built of wood at the Abeking & Rasmussen yard to a design by W. Starling Burgess, and many are still racing thanks to a timely conversion to fiberglass construction during the 1950s. Few other classes from the 1920s survive. As the author can testify from long experience, their long, full bows make them wet when banging into a sea and fast when running before one. Dimensions: length on deck 30' 6", waterline length 21' 6", beam 6' 6", draft 4' 9", sail area 385 square feet, displacement, 2 tons.

page 100, *Ticonderoga*, 1949

A speed record holder on several ocean races, the ketch *Ticonderoga* knocks off knots offshore. With the clipper bow, long bowsprit, and low sweeping sheerline, she is a flashback to *Fanny* and the other boats with which we opened this book. L. Francis Herreshoff, her designer, said of a boat of his with a similar look that she was "a great favorite of the sailormen as she is not at all tiresome to look at." He was once asked what an aspiring yacht designer should undertake in the way of training. In reply, he advised first attending art school to learn the rules of proportion. Unlike his father, Nathanael Greene Herreshoff, L. Francis believed that engineering and science could wait. The Quincy Adams yard launched *Ticonderoga* in 1936. Dimensions: length on deck 72' 6", waterline length 64', beam 16', draft 7' 11", displacement 54 tons.

page 101, International One Design 2, 1949

Sometimes all it takes to turn the heart is a single beauty spot. In 1937 sailors on western Long Island Sound learned as much after a man fell in love with a corner of a boat and caused them to go to the great bother and expense of replacing their old Sound Interclubs (page 76) with the new International One Design. Cornelius Shields one day spied a particular Norwegian International 6 Metre with a dainty stern. Smitten by that stern, he commissioned the Norwegian designer and builder Bjarne Aas to build a new, smaller boat around it. Shields became a missionary for the new boat, and so the Interclubs quickly became history. Despite their strange birth, the Internationals are fine boats that have long been raced in many large fleets in America and Europe— very aggressively, too, as proved by this photograph taken of one burrowing into a hard northwest wind. Dimensions: length on deck 33' 5", waterline length 21' 5", beam 6' 9", draft 5' 4", sail area 461 square feet, displacement 3.2 tons.

page 102, Lightning 2192, 1954

A Lightning Class sloop takes a gamble by splitting with the rest of the fleet in search of a little more air. This and other lightweight, inexpensive, centerboard boats that could be carried on trailers behind cars became extremely popular after World War II. The Lightning was designed in 1938 by Sparkman & Stephens and remains one of the most popular international classes. Dimensions: length on deck 19', waterline length 15' 10", beam 6' 6", draft 4' 11", sail area 177 square feet, displacement 700 pounds.

page 103, *Bolero*, 1954

The big yawl *Bolero* reaches off the line at the start of a race in the New York Yacht Club Cruise. Her owner is Commodore John Nicholas Brown, whom we saw at the helm of *Saraband* (page 85) and who named all his boats for dances. A conceptual development of *Baruna* (page 90), *Bolero* set the elapsed time record for the race from Newport to Bermuda. Brown had asked Olin Stephens for "an able cruising boat with a turn of speed" and what he got was this rapid beauty. Dimensions: length on deck 73' 6", waterline length 51', beam 15' 1", draft 9' 6", sail area 2,480 square feet, displacement 32. tons.

page 112, *Astrild*, 1931

An apt coda for a symphony of images of sleek yachts is this picture of a sloop named for the Norse goddess of love and pulled by a curvaceous genoa jib across a shimmering sea. Designed and built by Nathanael Greene Herreshoff in 1903, *Astrild* was later given a Marconi rig. Her dimensions in 1931: length on deck 48', waterline length 31' 7", beam 10' 6", draft 7' 4", sail area 1,425 square feet.

Photographers' Biographies

Arthur F. Aldridge, 1861–1923

After emigrating from England to the United States at the age of twenty-two, Aldridge had a long career as a sportswriter and photographer, specializing in boating. He wrote for several magazines and newspapers, served as editor of the *Rudder*, a prominent boating magazine, and at the time of his death was yachting editor for the *New York Herald*.

Charles E. Bolles, 1847–1914

Born in Philadelphia, Bolles established a portrait studio in Brooklyn in 1881. He also did maritime photography on New York Harbor, photographing commercial and naval ships as well as yachts. He covered all nine America's Cup matches (which were then sailed off New York) between 1881 and 1903, as well as many other races on the Atlantic coast and Lake Ontario. One of his photographs won a gold medal at the International Congress of Photography, held simultaneously with the 1900 Paris world's fair. Deeply concerned about artistic control over his images, he copyrighted each print and once brought suit against a publisher for copyright infringement. After his health deteriorated, he retired in 1907.

James Burton, 1871–1910

Burton arrived in New York from London in 1894. Whether he had been trained as a photographer is unknown, but by 1897 he had plenty of work. As a special photographer for *Harper's Weekly* and other publications, he traveled widely and covered the Spanish-American War in Cuba (where he was in combat), the world's fairs in Paris and Buffalo, a volcanic eruption in Martinique, a political convention in Kansas City, many football games and track meets, and other events. In 1897, one of his pictures was selected to illustrate a photography manual alongside an article by Alfred Stieglitz. He photographed yacht races, sometimes from the decks of the yachts themselves, often from small boats or stakeboats that provided the "spice and danger" he relished. In 1909, after the death of their child, his wife committed suicide. A year later, Burton shot himself.

Morris Rosenfeld, 1885–1968

Born in Austria, he came with his family to New York, where his father changed the family name from Rose to Rosenfeld. As a boy he entered a photo contest with a camera that he owned with some schoolmates and won the prize with a picture of a square-rigger at South Street. With the five-dollar prize he bought his own camera, and later dropped out of school to work for a photo engraver. He covered his first America's Cup match in 1899. After managing a portrait studio, he was a freelance photographer for newspapers and did darkroom work for several photographers. Rosenfeld set up his own shop on Nassau Street in lower Manhattan, purchased the photographic collections of Bolles, Burton, and other photographers, and while taking pictures of yachts did a considerable amount of commercial and industrial photography, often with a staff of more than a dozen and two busy darkrooms.

Stanley Rosenfeld, 1913–2002

Although the photo credit read "Morris Rosenfeld" during the founder's lifetime, his sons, William, David, and Stanley, took many photographs and handled the chase boat. Stanley succeeded his father as head of the firm (changing the credit to "Morris Rosenfeld & Sons"). He was raised in the Bronx, first worked at the office at the age of thirteen, and was obliged by the Great Depression to drop out of New York University to work full-time at the firm. While taking his own photographs, he often drove the firm's chase boat for his father. He wrote often about yachting history and the America's Cup, and edited a collection of images from the Rosenfeld Collection, *A Century Under Sail*. In 1984 he sold the firm's archives to the Mystic Seaport Museum, and later spent months at Mystic, cataloguing the Rosenfeld Collection.

Bibliography

PHOTOGRAPHERS

Arthur F. Aldridge
obituary, *New York Times*, October 24, 1923.

Charles E. Bolles
A. J. Peluso, Jr., "Charles E. Bolles: Photographer
of Yachts under Sail and Steam," *Maine Antique
Digest* (June 1990) and "The New York Maritime
Photographers," *The American Neptune* 58, no 1
(winter 1998); lawsuit, *New York Times* (June 16,
1895); obituaries, *New York Herald* (October 15, 1914)
and *Brooklyn Daily Eagle* (October 16, 1914).

James Burton
Burton, "Adventures of a Yacht Photographer,"
Country Life in America 4, no. 4 (August 1903) and
"Photographing Under Fire," *Harper's Weekly*,
(August 6, 1898); Charles H. Brown, *The Correspon-
dents' War: Journalists in the Spanish-American War*
(New York, 1967); obituaries, *New York Herald* and
New York Sun (January 14, 1910); tribute, *Yachting*
(March 1910): 218; *Who Was Who in America*, vol. 1.

The Rosenfelds
"Rosie Remembers," *Motor Boating* (August
1967); Morris Rosenfeld, *Sail-ho!: Great Yachting
Photographs* (n.p., 1947) and *Under Full Sail*
(Englewood Cliffs, N.J., 1957); Stanley Rosenfeld,
A Century Under Sail (Reading, Mass., 1984); John
Rousmaniere, "Looking for the One Shot: An
Interview with Stanley Rosenfeld," *WoodenBoat*
(September–October 1989); Morris Rosenfeld obitu-
ary, *Yachting* (December 1968); Stanley Rosenfeld
obituary, *New York Times* (December 25, 2002);
"A Cameraman Goes to Sea," *Literary Digest* 121
(January 25, 1936); Guy Gurney quote in *Scuttlebutt*
(December 31, 2002).

YACHT DESIGNERS

John G. Alden
Robert W. Carrick and Richard Henderson, *John G.
Alden and His Yacht Designs* (Camden, Me., 1983).

William Gardner
Scott Cookman, *Atlantic: The Last Great Race of
Princes* (New York, 2002); Francis Sweisguth,
"Biography of Mr. William Gardner," in Edwin J.
Schoettle, *Sailing Craft* (New York, 1928).

L. Francis Herreshoff
Jack A. Somer, *Ticonderoga: Tales of an Enchanted
Yacht* (Mystic, Conn., 1997).

Nathanael Greene Herreshoff
Maynard Bray and Carlton Pineiro, *Herreshoff of
Bristol* (Brooklin, Me., 1989); L. Francis Herreshoff,
Capt. Nat Herreshoff (New York, 1953).

A. Cary Smith
W. P. Stephens, *Traditions and Memories of American
Yachting* (Brooklin, Me., 1989).

Olin J. Stephens II
Stephens, *All This and Sailing, Too* (Mystic, Conn.,
1999) and *Lines* (Jaffrey, N.H., 2002).

Yacht Registers and Directories
The American Yacht List, Manning's Yacht Register,
and *Lloyd's Register of American Yachts*; Fessenden
S. Blanchard, *The Sailboat Classes of North America*
(Garden City, 1963); Francois Chevalier and Jacques
Taglang, *American and British Yacht Designs,
1870–1887*, 2 vols. (Paris, 1991), *America's Cup Yacht
Designs, 1851–1986* (Paris, 1987), and *J-Class* (London,
2002); Diana Eames Esterley, *Early One-Design
Sailboats* (New York: 1979); Luigi Lang and Dyer
Jones, *The 12 Metre Class* (London, 2001).

YACHTING HISTORY

Ed Holm, *Yachting's Golden Age* (New York, 1999);
Alfred F. Loomis, *Ocean Racing* (New York, 1936);
C. Stanley Ogilvy, *The Larchmont Yacht Club: A
History, 1880–1990* (Larchmont, N.Y., 1993); John
Parkinson, Jr., *The History of the New York Yacht
Club*, 2 vols. (New York, 1975); John Rousmaniere,
The Golden Pastime: A New History of Yachting
(New York, 1987) and *A Picture History of the
America's Cup* (Mystic, Conn.,1989); Edwin J.
Schoettle, *Sailing Craft* (New York, 1928); W. P.
Stephens, *Traditions and Memories of American
Yachting* (Brooklin, Me., 1989) and *The Seawanhaka
Corinthian Yacht Club: Origins and Early History,
1871–1896* (New York, 1963); New York Yacht Club
scrapbooks.

EVENTS

The America's Cup
John Rousmaniere, *America's Cup Book, 1851–1983* (New York, 1983) and *The Low Black Schooner: Yacht America, 1851–1945* (Mystic, Conn., 1987); Winfield M. Thompson and Thomas W. Lawson, *The Lawson History of the America's Cup* (Boston, 1902); quote, "The America's Cup, after all," *Yachting*, May 1910; quote, "With outstretched wings," Harold S. Vanderbilt, *On the Wind's Highway* (New York, 1939).

Canada's Cup
www.byc.com/ canadascup; *Outing's Monthly Review* (September 1896), online at www.aafla.org/Sports-Library/Outing/Volume_28/outXXVIIIo6/ outXXVIIIo6o.pdf.

Seawanhaka Cup
John Parkinson, Jr., *The Seawanhaka Corinthian Yacht Club: The Early Twentieth Century, 1897–1940* (New York, 1965); *Outing's Monthly Review* (September 1897), online at www.aafla.org/SportsLibrary/ Outing/Volume_30/outXXXo6/outXXXo6p.pdf.

Irolita and *Elena*
quote, "A Hard Fight," *Yachting* (June 1914).

HISTORY OF PHOTOGRAPHY

Daniel Finamore, *Encountering Poseidon: Photographic Encounters with the Sea* (Salem, Mass.: 1998); Beaumont Newhall, *The History of Photography* (New York, 1964); J. Horace McFarland, "The Photographing of Clouds," *Country Life in America* 4, no. 4 (August 1903); Alfred Stieglitz, "The Hand Camera—Its Present Importance," *The American Annual of Photography and Photographic Times Almanac* (1897).

YACHT AESTHETICS

Maynard Bray, "Reversing Curves: N. G. Herreshoff's Shape-Related, Hollow-Bowed Boats," *WoodenBoat* (September–October 1997); L. Francis Herreshoff, *The Common Sense of Yacht Design*, 2 vols. (New York, 1948); Llewellyn Howland III, "The Singular Beauty of Wooden Boats," *WoodenBoat* (September–October 1984); "Ornament in Yacht Design," *Yachting* (August 1915); Robby Robinson, "What Makes a Boat Beautiful?" *Sail* (October 1998).

EDITED AND PRODUCED BY CONSTANCE SULLIVAN

DESIGN AND TYPOGRAPHY BY KATY HOMANS

DUOTONE SEPARATIONS BY ROBERT J. HENNESSEY

PRINTED AND BOUND BY L. E. G. O., VICENZA, ITALY